Robert Merry

The Pains of Memory

A Poem

Robert Merry

The Pains of Memory
A Poem

ISBN/EAN: 9783337005788

Printed in Europe, USA, Canada, Australia, Japan

Cover: Foto ©Thomas Meinert / pixelio.de

More available books at **www.hansebooks.com**

THE

PAINS OF MEMORY.

A Poem,

BY ROBERT MERRY. A. M.

O Memory! thou fond deceiver,
  Still importunate and vain,
To former joys recurring ever,
  And turning all the past to pain:

Thou'rt like the world, the opprest oppressing,
  Thy smiles increase the wretch's woe,
And he who wants each other blessing,
  In thee must ever find a foe.

Goldsmith.

LONDON:

PRINTED FOR G. G. AND J. ROBINSON,

Pater-Moster Row.

1796.

The

PAINS

OF

MEMORY.

WHEN mournful evening's gradual vapours
   spread
O'er the dim plain, and veil the river's bed ;
While her own star with dull and wat'ry eye
Peeps through the sev'ring darkness of the sky ;
While the mute birds to lonely coverts haste,
And silence listens on the slumb'rous waste :

When tyrant frost his strong dominion holds,

And not a blade expands, a bud unfolds,

But nature dead, divested of her green,

Cloath'd in a solemn pallid shroud is seen :

When gather'd thunders burst, abrupt, and loud,

And midnight lightning leaps from cloud to cloud,

Or rends, with forceful, momentary stroke,

The ivied turret, and the giant oak ;

Can faint remembrance of meridian mirth,

Bedeck with visionary charms the earth ;

Renew the season when each wak'ning flow'r

Lifted its leaves to drink the morning show'r ;

Dispel the gloom, the fi'ry storm remove,

Gem the wide vault and animate the grove ?

The fond illusions could but feebly shew,

The colours scarce appear, or faintly glow,

Fix'd would the sad realities remain,

And memory waste her vaunted stores in vain.

Alas! all inefficient is her pow'r,

To cheer, by what is past, the present hour,

For ev'ry good gone by, each transport o'er,

She may regret, but never can restore.

Yet shall her fest'ring touch corrode the heart,

Compel the subjugated tear to start :

She calls grim phantoms, from the shad'wy deep,

And sends her furies forth to torture sleep :

The lapse of time, the strength of reason dares,

And with fresh rage her straining rack prepares.

Say, can the man, oppressed by grief, review

With tranquil eye the pleasures that he knew,

When in content, with love and friendship blest,

Their soft emotions charm'd his youthful breast;

And as he gave each wild idea scope,

Look'd to new joy with renovated hope?

Ah no! his thought with melancholy range,

Traces the progress of the afflictive change,

Adds to the immediate evil he endures,

By strong controul each struggling pang secures;

Till tir'd, and shock'd, he turns him in despair,

From things that have been, to the things that are.

For what avails it now that once his mind

Was light as air, and frolic as the wind,

Alike to sorrow or to vice unknown,

That ev'ry moral solace was his own,

Since at an alter'd season, mis'ry gave

Sighs for the past, and wishes for the grave?

How swiftly fly the raptures of our prime,

Swept by the tempest of destroying time,

Whose whirlwind lays the pride of empire low,

And mingles nature in a wild of woe!

Shall we then pond'ring on its varied rage,

By recollected bliss our cares assuage,

Expatiate freely on the ravag'd plain,

Where flow'd the stream, and wav'd the golden
grain,

Where fountains cool refresh'd the summer shade;

And hamlets gay diversified the glade,

Where show'd the sculptur'd fane its splendid site,

And groves, the grandeur of diurnal night?

Shall we not view the alter'd prospect rude,

With deep dismay, or chill solicitude,

And can the mind the sad reverse efface,

By fondly musing on each former grace?

Where'er we cast our retrospective eyes,

A waste of rocks, a dreary desert lies,

Here desolation's grasp has rent his flow'rs

That scatter'd fragrance round our infant bow'rs,

There the wide ruin of our hopes extends,

Mark'd with memorials of departed friends.

So the poor trav'ller from some alpine height,

Looks backward on his journey with affright,

For still the dangers past his thoughts confound,

And other dangers threaten still around;

The headlong precipice, the icy pass,

The whelming avalanche's monstrous mass,

The tumbling cliff, the torrent's sudden rise,

The tangled forest reaching to the skies,

The clust'ring clouds that wrap the mountain's side,
The frozen mists that o'er the valley glide,
These all in dread confusion strike his heart,
He fears to stay, nor ventures to depart.

Down in yon glade, beside that glassy pool,
There stands, and long has stood, the village school ;
Hark ! the gay murm'rings of the sportive train,
Free'd from restraint that gambol o'er the plain ;
List their shrill voices, and their bursts of glee,
Will future years recall their extacy ?
Perchance some one, hereafter, of the band,
From the brown summit of that jutting land,
Shall eye the well-known spot, the self same scene,
And the thin spire that peeps those groves between ;

Shall mark the peasant plodding as before,

And the trim housewife at the cottage door ;

Shall hear the pausing bell's pathetic toll,

Borne on the gale, announce the parting soul—

Of some old friend, who to his childhood kind,

Prepar'd the kite and stream'd it to the wind ;

Some busy dame, for cakes and custards known,

Who gave him credit when his pence were gone ;

Some truant ploughboy, who, neglecting toil,

Join'd him to seize the tempting orchard's spoil ;

Or in despite of peril, spread the snare,

As thro' the thicket pass'd the nightly hare ;

Then shall he think on all the woes of life,

His thankless children, or his faithless wife,

His fortune wasted, or his wishes crost,

His tender brother, sister, parents lost,

Till ev'ry object sinking into shade,
He sigh, and call oblivion to his aid.

The buxom lass who late secure from harm,
With gay importance bustled thro' the farm;
Tended her dairy at the break of dawn,
Or fed her circling poultry on the lawn;
O'er the wash'd floor, the cleanly sand let fall,
And brush'd the unseemly cobweb from the wall:
Who in the hay-time met the lusty throng,
And with her share of labour join'd her song,
To the faint reapers bore the humming ale,
Or jok'd the thrasher leaning on his flail;—
By vain ambition led at length to town,
In quest of fortune, and suppos'd renown,

c

If there, the victim of some worthless rake,

She chance its sickly pleasures to partake,

Mix'd with the pamper'd crowds, whose looks disclaim

The smile of virtue and the blush of shame;

Will she not oft regret the chearful day,

When sport and freedom hail'd the approach of May,

And many a rural pair beguil'd the hour,

With evening dance beneath the moonlight bow'r.

Or to her sad fate left, condemn'd to rove

The lawless paths of desultory love;

Will not her tortur'd bosom throb the more,

Whene'er she thinks on what she was before,

And finds recoiling from the insidious joy

A secret canker ev'ry rose destroy.

While all that memory's sorcery can dispense,
Shall add new pangs to loss of innocence.

From the dark east the yelling blasts arise,
And clouds on clouds roll dreadful thro' the skies ;
With sweeping fury the impetuous rain,
Bursts on the hills and murmurs o'er the main ;
Then to some promontory, bleak and bare,
Fierce as distraction, reckless as despair,
At night's cold noon, a tortur'd wretch retires,
Consum'd by memory's unrelenting fires ;
With smiling horror meets the piercing gale,
Waits the barb'd flash, and breasts the driving
    hail ;

While in his bosom with resistless force,

Rages the direr tempest of remorse.

And did'st thou, barbarous monster! did'st thou
dare

Consign to shame the violated fair;

To loathsome penury and death consign,

Her, whom thy flatt'ring tongue had call'd, divine?

Did'st thou not skill and artifice employ,

To lure the hapless maid, and then destroy?

What kind persuasion woo'd her soften'd sense,

What cunning falsehood, and what fair pretence,

What fond endearments, mingled with the kiss,

That promis'd constancy, and nuptial bliss!

And she did perish—yes, in yonder grove,

Seduced to vice, the sacrifice of love,

There on the chilly grass the babe was born,
Beneath that bending solitary thorn;
And there the infant's transient spirit fled,
And there the mother mingled with the dead.—
Then howl thy sorrows forth, unpitied rave,
Groan on the beach, or headlong seek the wave;
For never shall her wrongs from thee depart,
But thought revenge thy cruelty of heart.

The slave of guilt no cordial ever found
To dull the throbbings of her cureless wound,
The impressive contrast of anterior joys
With actual evils, ev'ry bliss destroys,
He now no more, as once, delighted views
Declining twilight melt in silv'ry dews;

No more the moon a soothing lustre throws,

To calm his care, and cheat him of his woes,

But winnow'd anguifh drops from zephyr's wing,

Veil'd is the sun, and desolate the spring,

The glitt'ring rivers sadly seem to glide,

And mental darkness shrouds creation's pride.

Nor vice alone, remembrance! dreads thy reign,

Virtue alike can sicken at thy pain.

Why does that drooping youth, with footsteps slow,

Pace the dark desert, or the vale of snow;

Why hold fantastic converse with the wind?

'Tis thou art with him, tyrant of the mind!

Lo! at thy call a beauteous nymph appears,

Trickt out in flow'rs, yet fainting with her fears;

A robe of white her polifh'd limbs conceals,

A burning blufh her secret woe reveals---

Again he views the gay procession move,

In all the mimic pageantry of love ;

Again beholds her at the altar's side,

Of age and avarice, the destin'd bride ;

Marks the grey spoiler smile with joy elate,

Hears the cold priest reratify her fate;

Forc'd by a parent's harfh decree to wed,

And bathe with endless tears the marriage bed.

Then, then thy scorching fires convulse his veins,

Her image settled on his thought remains ;

In ev'ry fhade her pensive form he sees,

Her wailing voice is heard in ev'ry breeze ;

He feels the pressure of her circling arms,

Traces her sweet redundancy of charms,

And still revolving on the dear display,
Sinks to the earth, in desolate dismay.

Long on those spreading hills, a rustic strove,
The wants of life, industrious to remove ;
Now bow'd the forest with continued toil,
Now forc'd the ploughshare thro' the obstructive
    soil ;
Or in his cottage plied some useful trade,
The hamlet's boast, the glory of the glade ;
And fondly hop'd a competence to raise,
The well-earn'd solace of his latter days.
But times of hard mishap, and wide distress,
Baffle his schemes, and make his little less,

Till driv'n at last from home, in want of bread,

On the damp sod he lays his aged head,

And as the cherish'd, vain ideas rise,

Shrinks from the gale, and in rememb'ring, dies.

But most to him shall memory prove a curse,

Who meets capricious fortune's hard reverse ;

Who once in wealth, indulg'd each gay desire,

While to possess, was only to require :

Who scatter'd bounty with a lib'ral hand,

And rov'd at will thro' pleasure's flow'ry land.

By ruin cast amongst the lowly crew,

What doleful visions pass before his view !

His taste, his worth, his wisdom disappear,

His virtues too, none notice, none revere:

D

Cold is the summer friend, who lov'd to trace

His playful fancy's ever-varying grace;

E'en nature's self a different aspect wears,

Dimm'd by the mists of slow-consuming cares.

Glows not a flow'r, nor pants a vernal breeze,

As in his hour of affluence and ease,

While ev'ry luxury that the world displays,

Wounds him afresh, and tells of better days.

Oft when the moonbeam penetrates the gloom

Of midnight, to the solitary tomb,

That holds the relics of a wife ador'd,

And his beloved children, *all* deplor'd,

A mourner hies, there defolately cast,

Woo's to his burning breast the hollow blast,

Welcomes the screech-owl's dirge, and rends his
　　hair,
Or half devout, half murm'ring, breathes a pray'r.
Then recollection to his eager sight
Conjures the shadowy semblance of delight,
Shows the fond partner of his blissful hour,
His infants sporting in the noontide bow'r;
By her again his social board is grac'd,
Upon his knees, the smiling cherubs plac'd;
O'er his charm'd ear again her accents creep,
To sooth his heart and tell him not to weep:
Her pitying gaze his deep despair reproves,
Fondly she counsels him who fondly loves,
And waves her snowy hand with tend'rest care,
Points his abode, and seeks to lead him there:

Till in a moment the delusion fled,
He drops a living corse upon the dead.

As the proud vessel o'er the ocean glides,
And seems to scorn the winds, and mock the tides ;
The jocund mariners expand the sail,
To seize the vigour of the viewless gale ;
From the high shrouds their carol'd ditties raise
To many a fav'rite maid, in notes of praise.
But now more sullen blows the perilous blast,
And the strong tempest works the struggling mast;
A moment *lulls*, and from the treach'rous pause,
Fresh horror gains, and fiercer fury draws ;
In vain the pilot shuns the o'erwhelming wave,
Useless the caution, for no skill can save ;

The timbers crack, the rudder quits its hold,

At random here and there the ship is roll'd.

Then comes the fiend of mem'ry to dispense

Amongst the crew, affliction's keener sense;

Dwells on each tender tie they left behind,

Grapples the soul, and preys upon the mind;

Shows the lorn wife distracted at their fate,

The weeping orphan's unprotected state,

Tells of the plighted virgin's ceaseless moan,

The faithful friend's dismay, the parent's groan,

And as to endless darkness down they go,

Clings to the last, and leaves the latest woe.

Observe yon structure stretching o'er the plain,

Sad habitation of the lost, insane!

Ha! at the grates what grisly forms appear,

What dismal shrieks of laughter wound the ear!

Heart-broken love the tenderest measure pours,

Sighs, and laments, incessantly adores;

Insatiate fury clanks his pond'rous chains,

Suspicious av'rice counts ideal gains;

Bewilder'd pride the swelling crest uprears,

And causeless penitence is drown'd in tears:

Wan jealousy, with scrutinizing glance,

On ev'ry side sees rival youths advance;

While maddest murder waits the sword to draw,

And ostentation flaunts in robes of straw:

Pale, piteous melancholy clasps her hands,

Sunk in deep thought, and as a statue stands;

Convulsive joy, imaginary state,

Low envy, ghastly fear, determin'd hate,

Loud agonizing horror, dumb despair,

And all the passions are distorted there.

Amidst those gall'ries drear, those doleful cells,

The unrelenting despot, mem'ry, dwells.

Fix'd on the burning brain, she urges still

Her ruthless pow'r, in mock'ry of the will;

Regretted raptures, long remember'd woes,

And ev'ry varying anguish, *she* bestows;

This is her sumptuous palace, these her slaves,

She reigns triumphant when the maniac raves.

But O! her victims feel the heaviest stroke,

Whene'er at intervals the spell is broke;

When casual reason is awhile restor'd,

And they themselves are by themselves deplor'd.

Behold the wretch who from that cavern flies,

Hell in his heart, destruction in his eyes ;

His bosom burns, his aggregated grief

Feeds on his being, and disdains relief;

Around he throws his solitary gaze,

Already dead to hope, and love, and praise ;

By sharp sensation wounded to the soul,

He ponders on the world,—abhors the whole ;

While black as night, his gloomy thought expands

O'er life's perplexing paths, and barren sands ;

In the dire workings of his wakeful dreams,

The human race a race of demons seems,

All is unjust, discordant, and severe,

He asks not mercy's smile, or pity's tear :

Guilt, hate, and horror drive him to the steep,

Reckless and fierce, he plunges in the deep ;

Breathes his rash spirit on the roaring tide,
And glories that he dies a suicide.
Alas ! he only strove to set him free
From thy abhorr'd dominion, memory !

Where are thy bounteous blessings, do they flow
On the blank current of preceding woe,
Or on a halcyon sea allure the sight,
In distant, floating bubbles of delight?
Small consolation from past ills we gain,
And comforts vanish'd, leave the sharpest pain.
From thee does gratitude for ever find
A settled bliss, a lasting ease of mind ?
Dost thou not come to dull it's sick'ning sense,
And many a secret murmur to dispense ;

To trace the benefactor's true intent,

And urge his selfish pride of sentiment,

Recal the gracious nod that follow'd soon,

The pitying smile as conscious of the boon,

Or bid it all at once indignant fly

From the keen sneer, the cold averted eye?

For heart-felt wrongs, thy stimulative force

Oft wakens vengeance, and impels its course;

Thy fev'rish hand lays bare each wound to view,

That it may throb, and rage, and bleed anew;

While all, perhaps, that virtue can acquire,

Is, not to pardon—but forget it's ire.

Afk the meek nun, who fled from wordly care,

Is doom'd to long involuntary pray'r;

To meagre fasts, and nights of broken rest,

With busy nature struggling in her breast :

Aſk, if she deem in her forlorn abode,

That sad seclusion is the will of God,

That her blue eyes so languishingly sweet,

Were meant to hide their lustre in retreat,

And dimm d with tears, eternally to trace

The dull, the holy horrors of the place :

Those glowing lips, with vermil dews o'erspread,

To kiss the mould'ring relics of the dead ;

The ear's vibration but to catch the swell

Nocturnal, of some melancholy bell ;

Unknown the thrilling extacies, that move

In the soft whisp'rings of the voice of love ;

The sense of feeling drawn o'er every part,

And all the fine emotions of the heart,

Were they bestow'd, a mournful wreck to lie
In the oblivious gulph of bigotry?
Her trembling tongue the motive would explain,
That fix'd her thus, alas, to live in vain.
Some dread remembrance of departed joy,
Beguil'd her reafon, pow'rful to destroy!
Left her like yonder leafless shrub to fade,
Hid from the light, and with'ring in the glade.

Thro' life's mysterious vale, from day to day,
Man, wretched pilgrim! journeys on his way;
Here tow'ring palaces attract his view,
There the lorn hovel shews it's tatter'd crew;
And if some casual flow'rs his senses greet,
Still rending brambles cling around his feet;

While, but a little onward, hangs the gloom
That hides the solemn precincts of the tomb:
Yet, lur'd by hope, a forward course he steers,
And shuns the painful retrospect of years.
For who, amongst the lowly, or the high,
His travers'd path with rapture can descry?
Some wild desire, some sad mistake has cast
Severe remorse, or sorrow on the past;
Some former fault shall present solace curb,
Or fair occasion lost his peace disturb;
Some fatal chance has ruin'd ev'ry scheme,
And prov'd his brightest prospects, but a dream.
E'en those, who by the million are confest,
The noblest, truest, wisest, and the best,
Shall in repining thanklessness declare,
They might have been far happier than they are;

And oft exclaim, " If time would but renew,

" How diff'rent were the system to pursue!"

Come then, creative fancy! hither bend

Thy sportive flight, and prove thyself a friend;

Raise by thy potent spells the castles fair,

Which charm the eye, though built but in the air;

Console the poor with visionary wealth,

And lure the sick man to the bow'rs of health;

To myrtle groves the panting lover bring,

And scatter roses from thy fairy wing;

The maid ador'd, though faithless as the wind,

Shall there be ever constant, ever kind,

With fond approval listen to his tale,

Melt at his sighs, and let his vows prevail.

Thou bidst the soldier win, with proud delight,
The deathless laurel of imagin'd fight,
Spur his bold steed the routed foe to reach,
Or foremost, sword in hand, ascend the breach.
Thy magic influence makes the coward brave,
Gives ease to anguish, freedom to the slave :
Yes, he alas ! condemn'd for evermore,
To tug with hopeless toil the heavy oar,
To guide the galley thro' the boist'rous sea,
In ev'ry hour of respite, flies to thee :
On the cold pallet stretch'd, his pangs subside,
O'er his rapt thought thy pageant pleasures glide,
Bright views entrance him, soft illusions rise,
Dissolve his chains, and lift him to the skies.
The niggard wretch at thy benign command,
Feels with new tenderness his soul expand,

Wakens to charity, and grants relief,

At least in thought, to ev'ry human grief;

Then, to reward his sympathetic tears,

Invokes prosperity, and length of years.

View'd thro' the medium of thy magic glass,

The loveliest scenes in gay succession pass,

Each virtue glows in purest tints array'd,

In native ugliness is vice display'd :

For never yet has mortal predesign'd

Himself unjust, deceitful, or unkind,

To gain the prize on which he loves to brood,

The means are proper, and the end is good.

Where'er thou deignst thy cheering glance to throw,

Full harvests bend, salubrious rivers flow,

Long lakes their glossy surfaces unfold,

And heaven is deck'd with more resplendent gold.

Spontaneous forests cloathe the lonely heath,

And all creation brightens at thy breath.

Then fancy, hither come, exert thy fway;

And chace the demon mem'ry far away !

Thou too, forgetfulness! whose opiate charm

Can hush the passions, and their rage disarm ;

Approach, O kindly grant thy suppliant, aid !

Wrap him in sweet oblivion's placid shade ;

Veil the gay, transitory scenes, that fled,

Like gleamy sunshine o'er the mountain's head ;

Sink in the dark abyss of endless night ;

The artificial phantoms of delight ;

Nor let his early ign'rance, and mistake,

The sober bliss of age and reason shake.

Hide from his heart each suff'ring country's woe,

And o'er its chains thy cov'ring mantle throw;

Hide yon deluded agonizing train,

Who bleed by thousands on the purple plain;

Their piercing cries, their dying groans controul,

And lock up all the feelings of his soul.

Shield him from slander's persecuting race,

Who seek to wound, and labour to disgrace,

Who view the humblest worth with jealous eye,

The viper brood of black malignity!

So shall, perchance, content with thee return,

'Mongst vernal sweets to raise his wintry urn;

To his retreat tranquillity repair,

" And freedom dwell a pensive hermit there."

O! in retirement may he rest at last,

The present, calm, forgotten all the past;

Beside the babling brook at twilight's close,

Taste the soft solace of the mind's repose;

List the lorn nightingale's impressive lay,

That soothes the evening of retiring May,

When the young moon her paly flag displays,

And o'er the stream the panting zephyr strays;

No heedless hours recall'd, no festive roar,

That once deluded, but can please no more;

No wild emotions bid his comforts cease,

Or from his cottage drive the angel peace;

Nor vain ambition tempt his thoughts anew,

But still preserve the friendship of the few;

Still, still preserve the fond domestic smile,

Of her, whose voice can ev'ry care beguile;

With meek philosophy his hours employ,

Or thrilling poetry's delicious joy;

And from the faded promises of youth,

Retain the love of liberty and truth.